I'm Going to be a Big Sister

Lindsey Coker Luckey

Copyright © 2018 Lindsey Coker Luckey

All rights reserved.

ISBN: 9781791782061

I'm going to be a big sister

And I don't know what to do.

Will my Daddy get rid of all of my toys,
Or paint my bedroom blue?

I will have to share my Mommy. It won't be just us three.

But will she love this baby

More than she loves me?

Mommy's tummy is growing

It's getting bigger every day.

The baby will be here soon.

Will I Still be able to play?

I love my Mommy and Daddy.

Will they have time for me?

Will I be all alone? Will they forget about me?

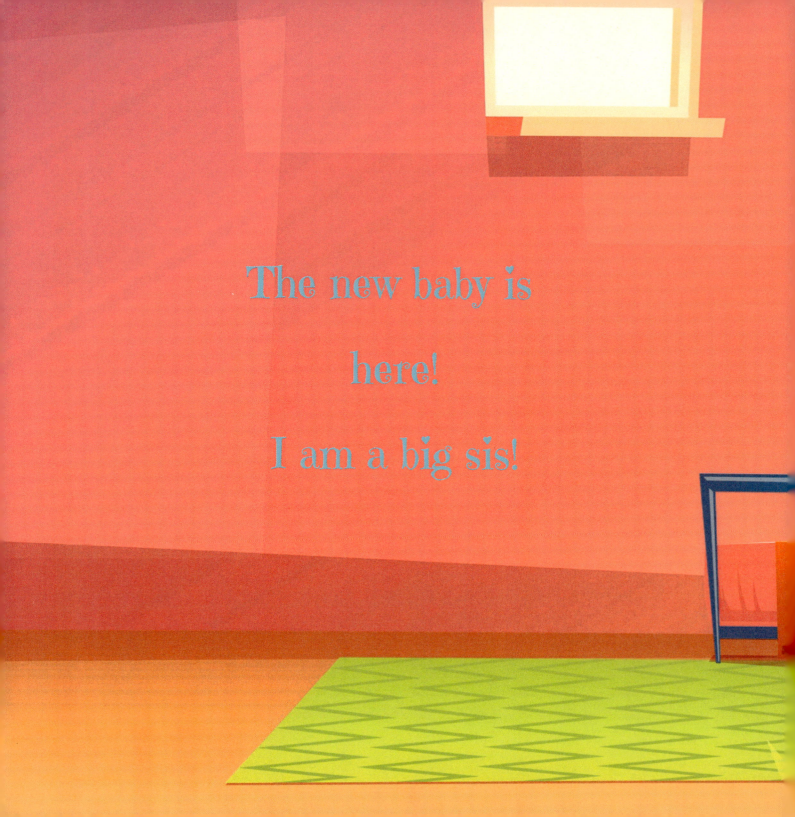

My new baby loves me. I can already tell.

I love the way baby skin

is so soft

And even how it smells.

I feel so silly

For being so scared.

I didn't know what to expect

And wasn't so prepared.

Mommy and Daddy

love me

Just as much as ever.

And now I have a new

baby

To be my best friend

forever.

See also:

Available on Amazon

Made in the USA
Lexington, KY
12 June 2019